*For my aunt Daisy Byam, who encouraged my storytelling voice – G. H.*

*In loving memory of Spot and Herman – J. C.*

First published in Great Britain in 2001 by
Frances Lincoln Limited, 4 Torriano Mews
Torriano Avenue, London NW5 2RZ

British Library Cataloguing in Publication Data
available on request

ISBN 0-7112-1850-1

Set in Adobe Garamond semi-bold

Printed in Singapore

1 3 5 7 9 8 6 4 2

# Sing Me a Story

## Song-and-Dance Tales from the Caribbean

### Grace Hallworth

### Illustrated by *John Clementson*

FRANCES LINCOLN

# Contents

# Author's note

Once I was telling a classful of infants a folk tale in which a song recurred throughout the story. The song words were preceded by the phrase, "And she sang ..." I began to speak the words of the song, and was immediately interrupted by a voice protesting, "But you aren't singing!" There was no melody provided, so I quickly borrowed the tune of a well-known nursery rhyme and the tale was transformed into an enjoyable shared experience, with everyone joining in the refrain.

During a regional festival, I shared the story "Dancing to the River" with a visiting infant school, and was delighted when all the teachers and parents spontaneously joined in the dance. Teenage boys in Buffalo, U.S.A. were equally keen to demonstrate their dancing talents only seconds after I told them them the story of a king who loved dancing so much, he invented a special dance – the Kokioko.

Most Caribbean folk tales originally came from Africa, where storytelling often includes chanting and singing, acting out and dancing. Children enjoy the repetitive chants and songs: it gives them a chance to be "in the story".

I hope that these five stories will soon have children and grown-ups on their feet singing a story and dancing a tale.

*Grace Hallworth*

## Glossary of Caribbean words

| | | | |
|---|---|---|---|
| *agouti* | small wild animal hunted in Trinidad | *dasheen* | a root vegetable |
| | | *dey* | there |
| *arepa* | a cornmeal pancake with spicy meat filling | *foreday* | the crack of dawn |
| | | *sapodilla* | a small tropical fruit |

# Dancing to the River

**Once upon a time** and a very long time ago, the animals of the forest set out to look for food.

The birds flew high above the trees, searching.

The squirrels dug up all their hiding-places, searching.

The monkeys swung from tree to tree, searching.

Not far away was a field with plenty of corn. When the animals and birds heard about the field, they rushed off to find it.

Turtle was paddling in the river. She saw the birds flying off. They flapped their wings, klak! klak! klak! It was quiet in the forest and Turtle was lonely, so she decided to follow them.

Turtle made her way along until she came to the large field. There she saw her friends stuffing themselves with ripe corn.

The birds called to Turtle, "Go away, Turtle! Watchman will catch you."

Turtle said, "Don't worry about me. I'll keep a sharp look-out for Watchman." But once Turtle was in the field, the corn was too high for her to keep a look-out.

Suddenly, there was Watchman, standing with a stick in his hand. The birds flapped their wings and flew away, klak! klak! klak! leaving Turtle all alone.

"Aha!" said Watchman. "Here's one thief who won't get away." He grabbed Turtle and put her in his bag.

As Watchman walked across the field he sang a calypso, with such a lively tune that Turtle's feet just itched to dance.

Now, Turtle loved dancing more than anything. So when she heard Watchman singing, she called out. "Hey, Watchman, that's a real sweet calypso, man!"

"You like my song? I make up the words, you know," said Watchman.

"I make up songs too," said Turtle.

"Well, why you don't make up a song for me now?" asked Watchman.

Turtle said, "But when I sing, I like to dance, and I need plenty of space."

So Watchman took Turtle out of the bag and placed her on the ground.

Turtle began to sing. As she sang, she made movements with her feet.

She danced to the right
and she turned around,

she danced to the left
and she turned around,

she leaped and she danced,
she twirled and she pranced,
she was dancing to the river.

This is what Turtle sang:

> Let's sing and dance to the tay-lay-lay,
> Let's turn and prance to the tay-lay-lay.
> Hear the music playing
> And the steel pan drumming,
> As we sing and we dance to the tay-lay-lay.

It was an easy tune to sing. It was a lively tune to dance to. Soon Watchman was dancing, too, shaking his shoulders and clicking his fingers.

He danced to the right and he turned around,
he danced to the left and he turned around,
he leaped and he danced,
he twirled and he pranced,
and he danced his way to the river.

Turtle danced faster and faster, and she took bigger and bigger steps.

Watchman tried hard to keep up with Turtle.

Turtle spun on her toes, she leaped and she twirled.

Watchman followed every spin and leap and twirl. He didn't notice where Turtle was heading, until he heard a loud SPLASH!

Turtle had dived into the river and swum away!

# Turtle's Song

Let's    sing    and    dance    to    the    tay- lay- lay,    Let's

turn    and    prance    to    the    tay - lay -    lay.

Hear the mu-sic    play- ing    And the steel pan drum-ming, As we

sing    and we    dance    to    the    tay - lay -    lay.

# Turtle's Dance

R = Right,  L = Left

The children stand in two facing rows, knees slightly bent, elbows bent at right angles to body.  All movements are made to the counts given at the end of each line.

## While song is sung for the first time

*Let's sing and dance to the tay-lay-lay*
Moving to R, twisting first heels together then toes together
(4 counts – heels, toes, heels, toes), flap hands from the wrist like fins, up and down.

*Let's turn and prance to the tay-lay-lay*
Repeat above, moving to L (4 counts).

*Hear the mu-sic play-ing  And the steel pan drum-ming*
Rising on to toes, turn around lifting alternate feet, and end facing the other row again. Raise hands in the air, flapping them like fins (8 counts).

*As we sing and we dance to the tay-lay-lay*
With feet still and hands on thighs, make 2 small knee bends.
On last 3 notes slap thigh 3 times.

## While song is sung for the second time

*Lines 1, 2 & 3:* Moving forward, and clicking fingers in time to the music, the facing lines cross and change places as follows:
With L toe touch R heel, then step forward on to L foot.
With R toe touch L heel, then step forward on to R foot. Repeat 8 times.

*As we sing and we dance to the tay-lay-lay*
Turn and repeat as before.

The rows of children are now facing each other as at the beginning of the dance, but on opposite sides.

# The Mermaid's Rock

**On the island of Jamaica** there is a tall cliff and at the foot of the cliff is a large pool where women gather every day to wash their clothes. But at night the pool is deserted, an eerie place full of mystery and foreboding. No one visits the pool at night except the foolhardy, and those who don't know the legend …

Folk say that at the edge of the pool there once stood a rough, white rock. On moonlit nights it glowed with an unearthly light. This rock, they say, was the throne of a mermaid called Dora, who used to sit combing her long, silky, green-tinted hair, humming softly to herself.

The tune she hummed was beautiful, yet haunting too. And although the song had no words, to all who heard it the meaning was clear: it was a promise that what they most desired would be granted to them.

When Dora heard someone approaching, she would dive into the pool, leaving her comb on the rock. From under the water she would sing her song:

*"Take my comb,*
*Return to your home*
*And I will come to you in your dream.*
*Take my comb,*
*Return to your home*
*And I will give you your heart's desire*
*Soo-oo-oooo-oon."*

Not far from the pool lived a girl called Hazel. Her father was a rich man and Hazel had everything she desired ... well, almost everything. For Hazel longed for hair that flowed down her back, hair that was as soft as the finest silk, hair that sparkled in the moonlight. She had tried everything – creams, oils, shampoos of all kinds, even garden herbs – all in vain. Sleeping and waking, she thought of nothing but long, silky hair. She spent nearly all her money travelling from one salon to another, from one city to another, from one continent to another, trying to find a magic treatment that would transform her hair and satisfy her longing.

Hazel knew the legend of the mermaid, but at first she didn't believe a word of it. However, after a while she thought to herself, "It can't do any harm to see whether the story is true." So one night she decided to walk to the pool.

As she approached, she heard the mermaid singing. Even as the sound chilled her to the bone, it captivated and drew her to the pool.

Dora heard footsteps and dived into the water, leaving the comb behind. The comb was so beautiful, it could only belong to a mermaid. Among its finely-carved teeth were a few silky strands of the mermaid's green-tinted hair.

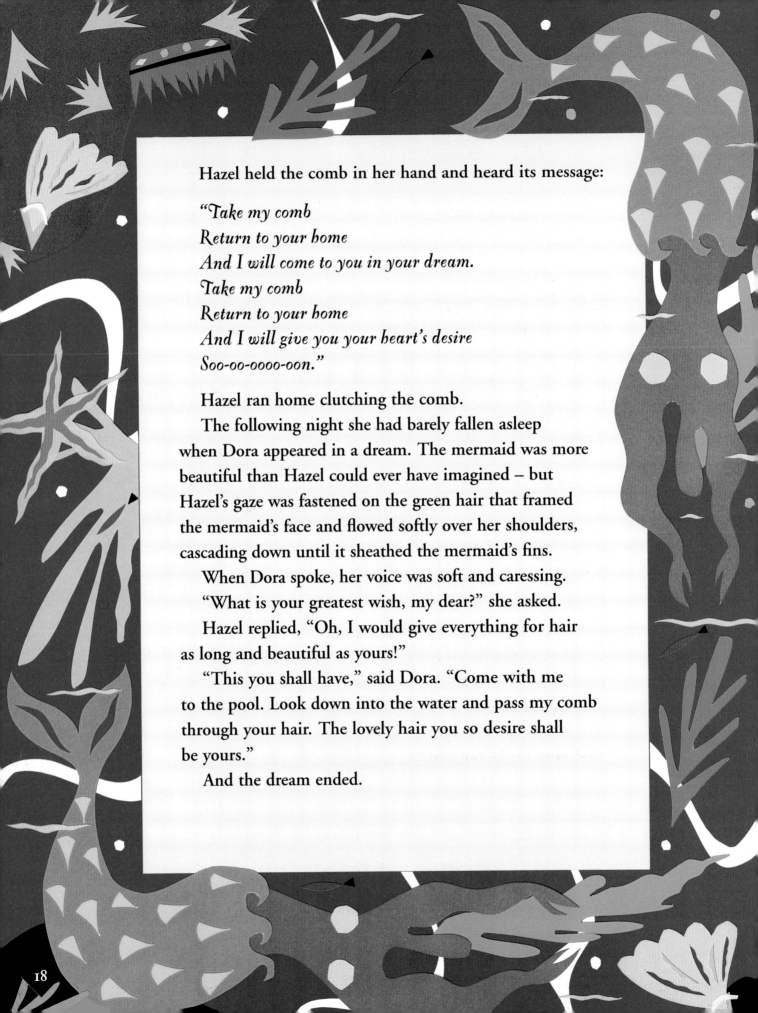

Hazel held the comb in her hand and heard its message:

*"Take my comb*
*Return to your home*
*And I will come to you in your dream.*
*Take my comb*
*Return to your home*
*And I will give you your heart's desire*
*Soo-oo-oooo-oon."*

Hazel ran home clutching the comb.

The following night she had barely fallen asleep when Dora appeared in a dream. The mermaid was more beautiful than Hazel could ever have imagined – but Hazel's gaze was fastened on the green hair that framed the mermaid's face and flowed softly over her shoulders, cascading down until it sheathed the mermaid's fins.

When Dora spoke, her voice was soft and caressing.

"What is your greatest wish, my dear?" she asked.

Hazel replied, "Oh, I would give everything for hair as long and beautiful as yours!"

"This you shall have," said Dora. "Come with me to the pool. Look down into the water and pass my comb through your hair. The lovely hair you so desire shall be yours."

And the dream ended.

Hazel awoke at once. There beside her was the mermaid's comb. She snatched it up and was out of bed in a trice, running to the pool.

When she got there, she scrambled up on to the rock and, looking down into the water, began to comb her hair. And each time she pulled the comb through, her hair was longer. Hazel saw that her hair now reached her neck, tickling it with such strangeness that she felt her blood curdle with cold. Soon her hair was flowing past her shoulders, and it was soft and brown like the tuft of hair at the end of an ear of full-grown corn. Soon it lay in thick tresses round her hips.

And now the rhythm of the combing became a command. "Comb! Comb! Comb!" As her hands obeyed, combing faster and faster, the hair grew longer and longer. As it grew, her neck bent towards the pool. She saw her hair spreading out on the surface of the water and, as it soaked up the water, it sank deeper and deeper, pulling Hazel, pulling, pulling.

Down, down, down, she bent until – SPLASH! The hair dragged her from the rock into the pool. Hazel tried to grab the rock, but her fingers slipped off its mossy green surface. She grasped at empty air, and sank to the bottom.

The next night Dora was back on the rock,
combing her hair and singing her wordless
haunting melody …

*" Mmmmmmm mmmm*

*mmmmmmmmmmmmm …"*

# Dora's Song

Take my comb_____ Re- turn to your home And

I will come to you in your dream. Take my

comb_____ Re- turn to your home And

I will give you your heart's de- sire Soo-oo- oooo- oon.

# Bouki Dances the Kokioko

**There was once** a king of Haiti who loved dancing, more than anything else in the world. If he could, he would have invited dancers to perform for him every evening of the week; but he did not have enough money in his treasury to pay them.

One evening after dinner, when the king was sitting alone in his garden, he made up a song:

*Kokioko, oh, Samba,*
*Now I dance, now I dance like this.*
*Samba, oh, Samba, ah.*
*Now I dance, now I dance like this.*
*Samba dance, Samba dance, Samba dance, Samba dance.*

He sang it several times, then sniffed the soft night air and, swaying from side to side, he made up a dance to match his song:

*Kokioko, oh, Samba,*
*Now I dance, now I dance like this.*
*Samba, oh, Samba, ah.*
*Now I dance, now I dance like this.*
*Samba dance, Samba dance, Samba dance, Samba dance.*

And the more he whirled around, the more impressed he was with his own dance.

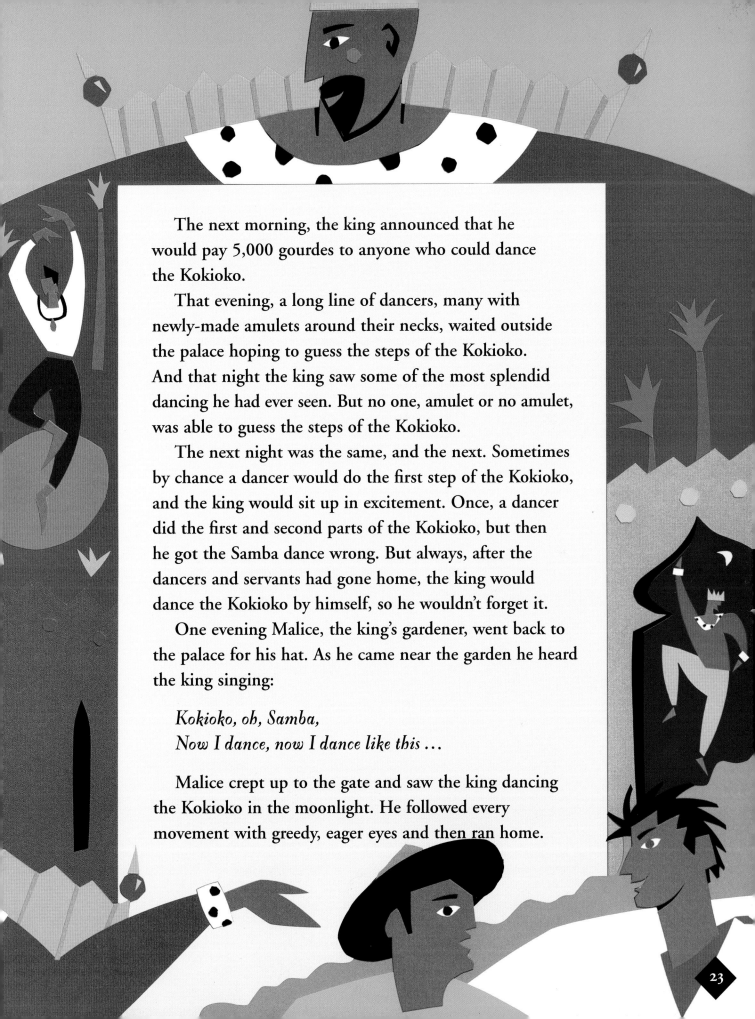

The next morning, the king announced that he would pay 5,000 gourdes to anyone who could dance the Kokioko.

That evening, a long line of dancers, many with newly-made amulets around their necks, waited outside the palace hoping to guess the steps of the Kokioko. And that night the king saw some of the most splendid dancing he had ever seen. But no one, amulet or no amulet, was able to guess the steps of the Kokioko.

The next night was the same, and the next. Sometimes by chance a dancer would do the first step of the Kokioko, and the king would sit up in excitement. Once, a dancer did the first and second parts of the Kokioko, but then he got the Samba dance wrong. But always, after the dancers and servants had gone home, the king would dance the Kokioko by himself, so he wouldn't forget it.

One evening Malice, the king's gardener, went back to the palace for his hat. As he came near the garden he heard the king singing:

*Kokioko, oh, Samba,*
*Now I dance, now I dance like this ...*

Malice crept up to the gate and saw the king dancing the Kokioko in the moonlight. He followed every movement with greedy, eager eyes and then ran home.

Before work the next morning, Malice went to see his friend Bouki.

"Bouki," he said, "we have been friends for many years, and now I am going to do something really great for you."

"Oh-oh," said Bouki. He knew Malice well enough to know that when Malice offered to help you … you were better off before than after he came along. No one was trickier than Malice.

"Bouki, do you know what I saw last night? I saw the king dancing the Kokioko. I watched every step. I can't dance it, because I am his servant and he would suspect me. But I will teach you the steps, and you can win the 5,000 gourdes."

Now 5,000 gourdes is a lot of money – especially for Bouki, who had many little Boukis to feed. And also for Malice – who had many little Malices.

"Show me the dance," said Bouki.

Malice sang and danced:

*Kokioko, oh, Samba,*
*Now I dance, now I dance like this.*
*Samba, oh, Samba, ah.*
*Now I dance, now I dance like this.*
*Samba dance, Samba dance, Samba dance, Samba dance.*

Then Bouki tried to follow Malice's movements:
*Koki-o-o-OH!*
Bouki was so fat and awkward, he nearly fell over.

"Never mind," said Malice, "I'll be back tonight to teach you. We'll learn a little bit more every night."

Two weeks later, Bouki and Malice joined the line of dancers waiting outside the king's palace. When it was Bouki's turn, he went in alone and danced for the king.

> *Kokioko, oh, Samba,*
> *Now I dance, now I dance like this …*

There was no doubt about it: it was the Kokioko. The king was amazed, and had to give Bouki his reward. Bouki rushed joyously out of the palace with his sack of 5,000 gourdes.

"I've won, Malice, I've won!" Bouki shouted.

Bouki and Malice walked gaily home through the forest, but as they passed a large breadfruit tree, Malice suddenly said "Bouki, now that you can dance the Kokioko, I'm going to teach you a much easier dance."

Malice moved his rump back and forth, closed his eyes and chanted:

> *If you have no sense,*
> *Put your sack on the ground*
> *And dance.*

"That's easy," said Bouki. He put his sack down and imitated Malice:

> *If you have no sense,*
> *Put your sack on the ground*
> *And dance.*

"Good," said Malice. And he began to chant faster and faster and shake his whole body:

> *If you have no sense,*
> *Put your sack on the ground*
> *And dance.*

Bouki did the same. And his eyes were shut tight when Madame Malice crept out from behind the breadfruit tree, picked up his sack and carried it off.

Suddenly Bouki opened his eyes and looked on the ground. "My sack, Malice, my sack! Where is it?"

"Oh-oh – did you put it on the ground?" asked Malice.

"Yes, of course."

"Oh Bouki ! I tried to warn you," said Malice. And he disappeared into the night, chanting:

> *If you have no sense,*
> *Put your sack on the ground*
> *And dance!*

# The King of Haiti's Song

Ko-ki-o- ko oh, Sam-ba,    Now I dance, now I dance like this.____ Ko- ki- o-

ko oh, Sam-ba,      Now I dance, now I   dance   like this.____        Sam-

ba __ oh _____      Sam- ba, ah _____ Sam-ba

dance,    Sam-ba dance,    Sam- ba    dance,    Sam-ba dance,    Sam- ba

dance,    Sam-ba dance,    Sam- ba    dance.  Sam-ba    dance

# The Kokioko

R = Right,  L = Left,  Up = on ball of foot,  Hip = stick out hip to R or L.

The children stand in a line, facing front, feet together, knees slightly bent, hands holding on to hips, thumbs in front, rest of fingers to the back.

*Ko-ki-o:* Stand feet together

*ko:* Lift R foot and tap Up

*oh:* Lift R foot and place flat to R side (feet are now apart)

*Sam-ba:* Hip R, Hip L

*Now:* Place R foot Up next to L foot

*I:* Left foot Up

*dance:* R heel down

*now I dance like this:* As for ko oh Samba, but starting with L foot.

Repeat sequence from the top starting with L foot.

*Sam-ba:* Hip R, Hip L

*oh————:* Clap rhythm, hands at L shoulder level

*Sam-ba:* Hip R, Hip L

*Ah————:* Clap rhythm, hands at L shoulder level

*Sam- ba dance*: Step forward on to R foot, L foot Up to R heel, step forward on to R foot at the same time flicking L foot Up and out to the back, and 1 clap (on the word *dance*) at R shoulder level. Repeat step, stepping forward with L foot. Clap is at L shoulder level.

Travel step like this moving anywhere in the space, so that the original line formation is broken up, and finish facing front to start the Kokioko again.

# Malice's Chant
## See instructions for the Kokioko

TRAVEL STEP:

*If you have no sense:* As if carrying a large sack over L shoulder, 1 travel step on to R foot, body upright.

*Put your sack on the ground:* Placing L foot down and bending forward to put sack down.

*And dance:* Hip R, Hip L. Hands on hips.

Repeat as many times as required.

# Quaka Raja

**There was once** a poor widow who lived in a hut at the edge of the forest with her four children. She loved her three daughters – Minnie Minnie, Minnie Bitana and Philambo – but did not care a wit for her son Quaka Raja.

Quaka Raja worked hard in the vegetable garden while his three sisters quarrelled and fought all day. They made fun of Quaka because he was kind to the birds and animals of the forest, and always saved some of his food for them.

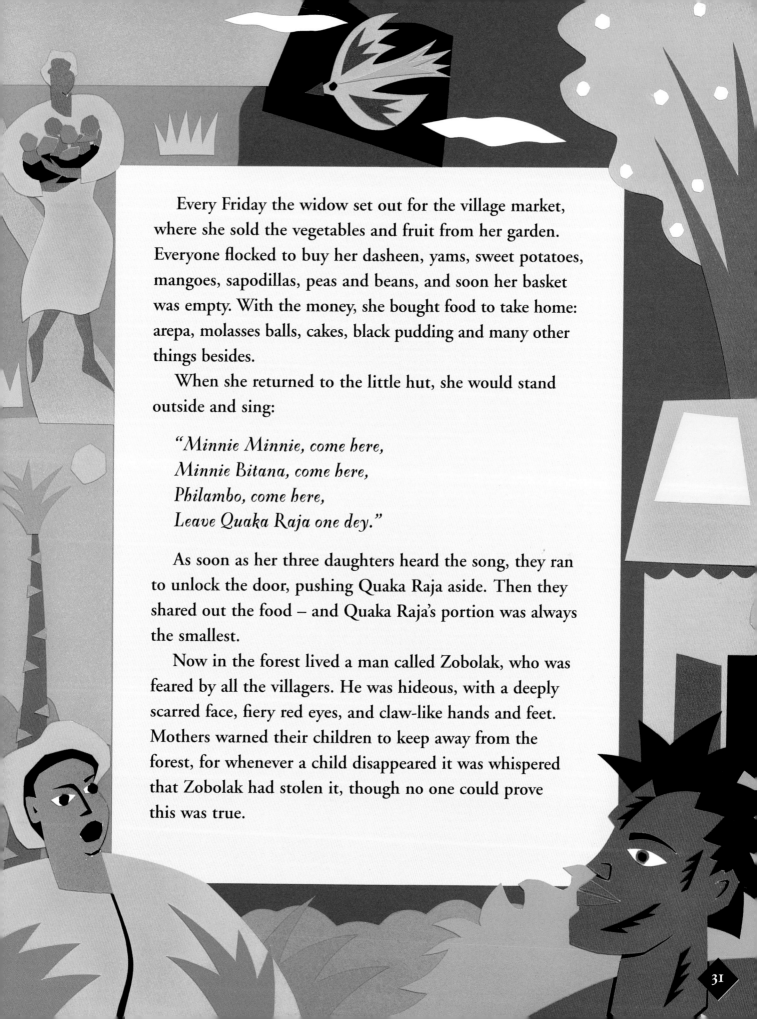

Every Friday the widow set out for the village market,
where she sold the vegetables and fruit from her garden.
Everyone flocked to buy her dasheen, yams, sweet potatoes,
mangoes, sapodillas, peas and beans, and soon her basket
was empty. With the money, she bought food to take home:
arepa, molasses balls, cakes, black pudding and many other
things besides.

When she returned to the little hut, she would stand
outside and sing:

*"Minnie Minnie, come here,*
*Minnie Bitana, come here,*
*Philambo, come here,*
*Leave Quaka Raja one dey."*

As soon as her three daughters heard the song, they ran
to unlock the door, pushing Quaka Raja aside. Then they
shared out the food – and Quaka Raja's portion was always
the smallest.

Now in the forest lived a man called Zobolak, who was
feared by all the villagers. He was hideous, with a deeply
scarred face, fiery red eyes, and claw-like hands and feet.
Mothers warned their children to keep away from the
forest, for whenever a child disappeared it was whispered
that Zobolak had stolen it, though no one could prove
this was true.

One Friday, when the widow returned from market, Zobolak, who had been hunting agouti, happened to be nearby. Peeping through the bushes, he heard the widow's son working and saw the three daughters run out to greet their mother. Zobolak could hardly restrain himself from seizing the three girls then and there, but he was as cunning as the wild animals he hunted. He settled down to wait.

The next Friday, when the widow had gone to market. Zobolak crept up to the hut and sang in a high voice:

*"Minnie Minnie, come here,*
*Minnie Minnie, come here,*
*Minnie Minnie, come here,*
*Leave Quaka Raja one dey."*

The three daughters ran to open the door but Quaka Raja said, "Sisters, sisters, don't go out. That is not Mamma's song." And he stood in front of the door and would not let them out, even though they tugged and pulled until they were exhausted.

When the children did not open the door, Zobolak hid nearby until the mother returned, and listened carefully to her song.

The following Friday, the mother set off once more, and Zobolak crept up to the hut and sang in a high voice:

*"Minnie Minnie, come here,*
*Minnie Minnie, come here,*
*Philambo, come here,*
*Leave Quaka Raja one dey."*

Once more the three daughters ran to unlock the door, but Quaka Raja said, "Sisters, sisters, don't go out. That is not Mamma's song." They tugged and pulled and scratched him, but he stood fast in front of the door, and at last they fell down exhausted.

Once more Zobolak crept away, but waited close by until their mother returned

At last Friday came. Zobolak's eyes gleamed with excitement as he waited. No sooner had the widow left, than he crept up to the hut and sang in a high voice:

*"Minnie Minnie, come here,*
*Minnie Bitana, come here,*
*Philambo, come here,*
*Leave Quaka Raja one dey."*

Quaka Raja stood in front of the door and begged his sisters not to go out. Their mother had just left, he told them, so how could she be back so soon? But they tugged and pulled and kicked so hard that he fell to the ground senseless.

Then they ran out to greet their mother, but – "Ayayayayay!" – there was Zobolak waiting for them. He threw them into his sack, slung it over his shoulder, and off he went to his den in the forest.

By the time Quaka Raja came to his senses, Zobolak was far away. Quaka Raja ran everywhere calling his sisters, but only the birds cheeped back at him.

When his mother returned from the village and he told her what had happened, she was wild with grief. But Quaka Raja said, "Don't cry, Mamma, I will go and look for my sisters and bring them back to you."

At first his mother begged him not to go. But Quaka Raja pleaded with her until she agreed. So she packed him some food and sent him off with tears in her eyes.

Quaka walked long and far. He walked all day, and as night fell he saw a light in the distance. Then he came to a hut half-hidden by trees and creepers. Inside he could hear his sisters crying.

What to do now? He could not rescue them without help. As he stood thinking, an owl hooted overhead.

At that moment he thought of a plan. He would ask his
friends, the birds and animals of the forest, to help him.
   Later that night, the stillness of the forest was shattered
by a terrible noise. Zobolak was startled out of his sleep
as the sounds grew louder and nearer, like the shrieks of
a hundred demons. He rushed out of his hut and ran deep
into the forest, over the mountains – anywhere to get away
from that horrible noise.

What was the noise? It was owls hooting, frogs croaking, wild cats yowling, wild pigs snorting and grunting, parrots screaming and birds chirping and whistling. They had all come to help Quaka Raja.

So Quaka Raja returned home with his sisters, and his mother was so proud of him that if he wasn't such a sensible son, he would have been thoroughly spoiled.

And for all we know, Zobolak is still running!

# The Widow's Song

Min-nie Min-nie, come here, Min-nie Bi- ta- na, come here, Phil- am-

bo, come here, Leave Qua- ka Ra- ja one dey.

# Tiger Dances to Turtle's Tune

**Tiger owned a large farm** on which he grew fields full of crops.

At harvest time he needed help to reap the crops – but mean old Tiger didn't want to pay wages. So he visited each of his neighbours and said, "This Saturday my wife and I will be doing a big cook-up. There'll be wild meat, roasted yams and sweet potatoes and plenty to eat and drink, in exchange for a little help on the farm."

The neighbours knew what a sweet-hand cook Madame Tiger was. Of course they agreed to help – all except Turtle, who wasn't invited.

"Who needs a small, weak creature like Turtle!" declared Tiger, when they reminded him that Turtle hadn't been invited.

Bad news travels fast. Turtle heard about the feast, and she heard what Tiger had said about her.

"We'll see about that," Turtle said to herself.

She went to see her good friend Armadillo, and asked him to help her dig a tunnel alongside the road going from Tiger's farm to his house.

When Saturday came, Turtle waited in the tunnel.

On Saturday morning, the workers began turning up on Tiger's farm. They worked hard to get most of the reaping done before the scorching afternoon heat.

When all the harvest had been gathered in, Tiger said to one of the men, "Go tell my wife and daughter to bring out food for the feast."

The man set off, and on his way he heard music. Someone was playing a guitar and singing a song. It went like this:

*Everyone working for Tiger today,*
*All the neighbours come here to work since foreday,*
*But Tiger, he singing hip hurrah! hip hurray!*
*'Cos they giving their labour, but he don't have to pay!*

*See how they digging,*
*Some of them pulling,*
*And then they picking,*
*But they have to jump, jump, jump!*

It was such sweet music that the man forgot all about the food and drink. His feet itched to dance.
Soon he was dancing and moving his feet this
way and that way ...
moving his hands this way and that way ...
and his body this way and that way ...
and he was jumping high, high, high, and singing,

*Everyone working for Tiger today,*
*All the neighbours come here to work since foreday ...*

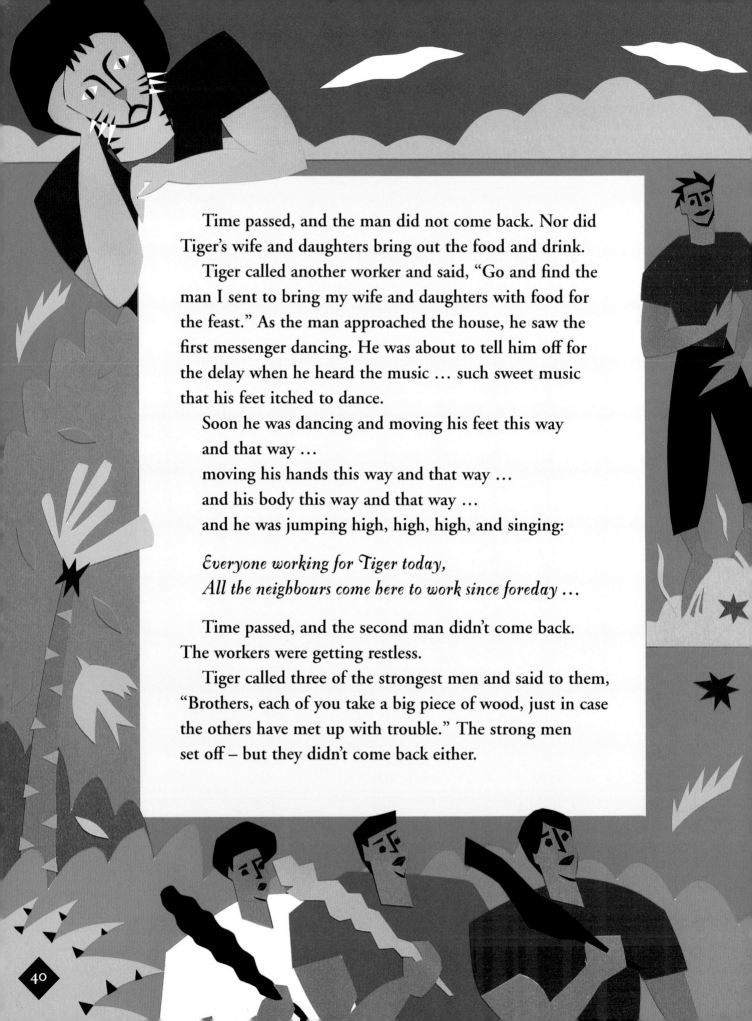

Time passed, and the man did not come back. Nor did Tiger's wife and daughters bring out the food and drink.

Tiger called another worker and said, "Go and find the man I sent to bring my wife and daughters with food for the feast." As the man approached the house, he saw the first messenger dancing. He was about to tell him off for the delay when he heard the music … such sweet music that his feet itched to dance.

Soon he was dancing and moving his feet this way and that way …
moving his hands this way and that way …
and his body this way and that way …
and he was jumping high, high, high, and singing:

*Everyone working for Tiger today,*
*All the neighbours come here to work since foreday …*

Time passed, and the second man didn't come back. The workers were getting restless.

Tiger called three of the strongest men and said to them, "Brothers, each of you take a big piece of wood, just in case the others have met up with trouble." The strong men set off – but they didn't come back either.

Meanwhile, Tiger's wife and daughters had set out with the food and drink. They were walking back along the road to the farm, when they heard music ... such sweet music that their feet itched to dance. At once they put down their trays and began to dance.

Soon they were twisting their feet this way and that way ... moving their hands this way and that way ... and their bodies this way and that way ... and they were jumping high, high, high, and singing:

*Everyone working for Tiger today,*
*All the neighbours come here to work since foreday ...*

Tiger had waited long enough. He and the workers set out for the house. They had only gone a little way when they saw Madame Tiger, her daughters and the five men prancing and dancing.

Tiger was furious! But no sooner did he hear the music, such sweet music, than he and the workers all began to dance and sing:

*Everyone working for Tiger today,*
*All the neighbours come here to work since*
*foreday ...*

41

Suddenly Tiger realised what he was singing – and stopped. The workers stopped too.

Then Turtle came up out of his tunnel.

"Turtle!" exclaimed Tiger. "Why you do this to me?"

"Tiger, I may be small and weak," said Turtle, "but I'm clever enough to get your workers to join *my* party, even though all I can give them is music."

Tiger was so ashamed that he invited Turtle to share the delicious meal his wife had prepared for the harvest celebration. And Turtle accepted the invitation, so there was not only food and drink, but sweet, sweet music to dance the day away!

# Turtle's Tune

E- ve- ry- one work- ing for Ti- ger to- day,

All the neigh-bours come here to work since fore- day, But

Ti- ger, he sing-ing hip hur- rah! Hip hur- ray! 'Cos they

gi- ving their la- bour, but he don't have to pay!

See how they dig- ging, And some of them pul- ling,

And then they pick- ing, But they have to jump, jump, jump-jump!

# Tiger's Dance

R = Right  L = Left

BASIC STEP:  a stamping walk accompanied by arm movements.

A.     Digging earth with a large garden spade and throwing away across body to L.

B.     Holding a rope with both arms outstretched in front at waist level and pulling towards body.

C.     L arm as if holding a basket on L hip, R arm picking an orange off an overhead branch and putting it into basket.

H.     Hurrah gesture: arms at shoulder level, fists loosely clenched, then shooting arms up above head splaying out fingers.

The children stand in a large circle, R shoulder towards centre.  Start stamping walk with R foot, using gesture A. – digging, moving to the R.

*E-ve-ry-one work-ing for Ti-ger to-day*

A.     Dig - throw - dig - throw

B.     Hold - pull - hold - pull

C.     Pick - basket - pick - basket

*All the neigh-bours come here to work since fore-day*

A.     Dig - throw - dig - throw

B.     Hold - pull - hold - pull

C.     Pick - basket - pick - basket

*But Ti-ger he sing-ing hip hur-rah Hip hur-ray*

Fist open - fist open - fist open - fist open

Repeat each time song is sung

*'Cos they giv-ing their la-bour, but he don't have to pay*

A.     Dig - throw - dig - throw

B.     Hold - pull - hold - pull

C.     Pick - basket - pick - basket

*See how they dig-ging*

A.     Dig - throw

*And some of them pul-ling*

B.     Hold - pull

*And then they pick-ing*

C.     Pick - basket

*But they have to jump jump jump-jump*

Jump, feet together, ¼ turn to R on each 1, 2, 3, 4

with arms above in Hurrah gesture, to end with R shoulder

again towards centre.

Repeat song with gesture B – pulling

Repeat again with gesture C – picking